Minnesota in Focus

Minnesota in Focus

Text by
George Moses
Photographs
by *The
Minneapolis
Star* and the
*Minneapolis
Tribune*

*University of Minnesota
Press, Minneapolis*

The Minneapolis Star and the *Minneapolis Tribune*
assisted in the publication of this book.

Library of Congress Catalog Card Number: 74-79504

ISBN 0-8166-0718-4

Preface

This book grew out of a desire to publish a fresh view of the Minnesota of today. To make it possible, *The Minneapolis Star* and the *Minneapolis Tribune* offered the full resources of their photographic library. And it fell to me, as one who had spent twenty years traveling in and writing about the state, to put the book together.

An introduction, as I understand it, should say what the book is, what it isn't, give thanks to those on whom it leans heavily, and make clear that if anything in the book is fuzzy or incorrect, the writer alone is to blame. Fair enough.

The heart of this book is the more than two hundred photographs, nearly one-third of them in color, which mirror contemporary Minnesota. They were taken by twenty-nine present and former *Star* and *Tribune* photographers, mostly during the two or three years before the book was published.

They show Minnesota in many moods — in summer, in winter, at work, at play. They capture moments of pleasure, of tension, and of humor. And many of them, from all parts of the state, reflect the artistry and sense of beauty that belong to the best of news photographers.

In presenting a collection of photographs — especially one which draws on as large a storehouse as this book does — it's something of a cliché to say that the winnowing-out process was difficult. And so it was. During my years as Associated Press bureau chief in Minneapolis (a position that took me regularly to all areas of the state), I worked with and came to know well many of these photographers. In fact, when the picture selection began, I remembered, looked for, and found certain prints I knew ought to be included.

The book, we decided, would treat Minnesota in three ways — first, from an overall view as a state that has developed in its own individualistic way; second, as a producer of wealth; and third, as one of the nation's most favored playgrounds. This decision simplified the process of selection somewhat, but the job of discarding four out of every five of the pictures we considered remained difficult. In this, and in the entire planning and layout of the book, the skilled hand of Robert Taylor, University of Minnesota Press designer, is evident. So, in a less visible way, are the many hours spent by Elaine Jenson, assistant *Star* and *Tribune* librarian, in searching the files for various kinds of photographs. Time and time again Chief Librarian Robert Lopez and others on the library staff also facilitated the work.

The photographers themselves, representatives of a team whose work has won more than four hundred prizes in the last twenty-five years, went out of their way to help on picture details and, sometimes, to recall photos illustrating a certain desired theme. Chief Photographer Earl Seubert of the *Tribune* was particularly generous with his time and suggestions.

Many years as an observer of my adopted state had equipped me with some perspectives on Minnesota when I began to knit these pictures together with words. I supplemented them with more detailed reading and study of Minnesota than I had managed in all my time as a journalist. I sought out many institutions, public and private, to augment, modify or, in some cases, nullify my own concepts. It was possible to include in these pages only a tiny fraction of the research assembled, and some persons who went well out of their way to help me will not find their work recognizable here. But it was all invaluable as background, and it is all appreciated.

This book does not presume to be an encyclopedia of Minnesota. It pictures only briefly, or not at all, many places and institutions which have helped give the state its distinctive flavor, among them the lively, distinguished, and innovative cultural scene centered in the Twin Cities.

And there are many pictures of Minnesota that exist only in my memory. They are not — with all respect to the discerning and far-ranging *Star* and *Tribune* photographers — in the files. For instance, the little farmhouse on a quiet country road near Austin one December. It needed paint, but its owner had chosen instead to decorate it with strings of blazing Christmas lights, as if his home sat on a well-traveled suburban street. Or the load of red potatoes with bits of black dirt clinging to them as they spilled over a truck en route to East Grand Forks during the Red River valley harvest.

Or the time when, rushing to a now-forgotten evening appointment somewhere in northern Minnesota, I fell in behind a horse-drawn wagon in a no-passing zone. At three or four miles an hour, there was time to glance around and to see what I would otherwise have missed: a shaft of light from the setting sun brightening a little pond where a family of ducklings swam and an antlered deer had come to drink on the farther shore.

To the Minnesota it only suggests, as well as to the Minnesota it shows, this book is dedicated.

G. M.

Macalester College, 1974

Contents

Picture Credits

Photographs are listed by page number. Unless otherwise indicated, the order is top to bottom or left to right.

2. Mike Zerby.
10. Duane Braley.
13. Pete Hohn; Earl Seubert.
14. Earl Seubert; Larry Schreiber.
15. Not identified.
16. John Croft; Kent Kobersteen.
17. John Croft; Duane Braley.
18. Earl Seubert.
19. Earl Seubert.
20. Earl Seubert.
21. Earl Seubert.
22. Jerry Brimacombe.
23. Earl Seubert.
24. Charles Bjorgen; Regene Radniecki.
25. Don Black; Kent Kobersteen.
26. Above, Earl Seubert; below left, Wayne Bell; below right, not identified.
28. Earl Seubert.
29. Earl Seubert.
30. Above left, Lee Hanley; above right, not identified; below, Jim Kimball.
31. Kent Kobersteen.
32. John Croft; Skip Heine.
33. Larry Schreiber.
34. Dwight Miller.
35. Mike Zerby.
36. Earl Seubert.
37. Richard Olsenius.
38. Above, left and right, Charles Bjorgen; below, William Seaman.
39. Earl Seubert.
40. Earl Seubert.
41. Regene Radniecki.
42. Earl Seubert; Powell Krueger.

43. Above left, Kent Kobersteen; above right and below, William Seaman.
44. Kent Kobersteen.
45. Skip Heine.
46. Above left and right, Earl Seubert; below, Pete Hohn.
47. Earl Seubert.
48. John Croft.
49. Earl Seubert; Richard Olsenius.
50. Richard Olsenius; Joe Hennessy.
51. Earl Seubert.
52. Jack Conner.
53. Duane Braley; Earl Seubert.
54. Earl Seubert; Richard Olsenius.
55. Earl Seubert.
56. Earl Seubert.
57. Bonham Cross.
58-59. Kent Kobersteen.
60-61. Mike Zerby.
62. Mike Zerby; Skip Heine.
63. Duane Braley.
64. Earl Seubert; Duane Braley.
65. Earl Seubert.
66. Earl Seubert.
67. Earl Seubert.
68. Earl Seubert.
69. Richard Olsenius; Kent Kobersteen.
70. Earl Seubert.
71. Earl Seubert.
72. Richard Olsenius.
74. Earl Seubert.
77. John Croft.
79. Earl Seubert.
80. Kent Kobersteen.
81. Earl Seubert; W. Allen Royce.
82. Not identified; Powell Krueger.

83. Charles Bjorgen.
84. Kent Kobersteen; Duane Braley.
85. Earl Seubert.
86. John Croft.
87. Earl Seubert.
88. Richard Olsenius.
89. Duane Braley.
90. Earl Seubert.
91. Earl Seubert.
92. Ben Kern; Earl Seubert.
93. Pete Marcus; Powell Krueger.
94. Earl Seubert; Powell Krueger.
95. Mike Zerby; Earl Seubert.
96. Earl Seubert.
98. John Croft.
101. Don Black.
103. Earl Seubert.
104. Earl Seubert.
105. Richard Olsenius.
106. Richard Olsenius.
107. Richard Olsenius.
108. Kent Kobersteen.
109. Kent Kobersteen.
110-111. Earl Seubert.
112. Earl Seubert.
113. Earl Seubert.
114. Earl Seubert.
115. Earl Seubert.
116. Earl Seubert.
117. Not identified; Earl Seubert.
118-119. Earl Seubert.
120. Earl Seubert.
121. Earl Seubert.
122. Ralph Thornton.
123. Earl Seubert.
124. Roger Nystrom.
125. Earl Seubert.
126. Earl Seubert.
127. Kent Kobersteen.
128. Regene Radniecki; Pete Hohn.

129. Kent Kobersteen.
130. Ben Kern.
131. Kent Kobersteen; Dwight Miller.
132. Earl Seubert.
133. Kent Kobersteen; Larry Schreiber.
134. Earl Seubert.
135. Jack Gillis; John Croft.
136. Jack Gillis.
137. John Croft; Earl Seubert.
138. Left, Kent Kobersteen; above right, Ben Kern; below, Jim Kimball.
139. John Croft; Earl Seubert.
140. Ben Kern.
141. Kent Kobersteen.
142. Wayne Bell; Mike Zerby.
143. Earl Seubert.
144. Kent Kobersteen; John Croft.
145. Earl Seubert; Wayne Bell.
146. Earl Seubert.
147. John Croft.
148. Duane Braley; Larry Schreiber.
149. John Croft.
150. John Croft; Mike Zerby.
151. Earl Seubert.
152. Earl Seubert.
153. Don Black; Earl Seubert.
154. Earl Seubert.
155. Above, Charles Bjorgen; below left, Earl Seubert; below right, Richard Olsenius.
156. Bill Davis; John Croft.
157. Earl Seubert.
158. Duane Braley.
159. Roger Nystrom.
160. Mike Zerby.

The Land and the People

The Land and the People

Minnesota is really two states. One is the Twin Cities of Minneapolis and St. Paul plus their suburbs, an urban conglomerate where more than half the people of the state live without feeling they're unduly crowded. Here are the ingredients of a metropolis — the tall buildings, the financial centers, the big league sports, the billion-dollar industries, the sky filled with jet planes, the university campuses, the artists, the thinkers, the leaders, the planners.

The other state is the rest of Minnesota — farms and forests and lakes, predominantly small towns — with a kind of deep-seated suspicion, sometimes tinged with envy, about the way people carry on in the Twin Cities.

Interdependence is admitted, and both sections furnish plenty of loyalists who can sing the state hymn with prideful gusto at University of Minnesota football games in Minneapolis. But the city dwellers, although aware of their dependence on the grain, the milk, the iron, and the lumber of rural Minnesota, sometimes feel that the main goal of rural legislators at the capitol in St. Paul is to impede the cities' efforts to solve their urban growing pains. And the outstate residents are inclined to feel that the Twin Cities, steadily growing while much of the state is losing population, are bent on prospering still more at the expense of the rural areas.

Consequently, rural Minnesotans who share this view but who are also sports fans observed with mixed emotions the big professional sports explosion of the 1960s. Entering the Twin Cities in rapid order were big league baseball (the Minnesota Twins), big league football (the Minnesota Vikings), and big league hockey (the Minnesota North Stars). The muscled gods these fans had known only on television were now going to sweat and bleed right here in Minnesota.

Of course, to see the pros would mean coming to the Twin Cities, and this, for some, was the catch. More than one suspicious outstater regarded the blossoming of major league sports as less a calculated move by team owners than another Twin Cities plot to bring the fans and their dollars in from the country. The fans came anyway.

Yet the Twin Cities aren't all this separate and homogenized a section of the state, and the point was never made more clearly than by this same sports explosion. Though separated by only the Mississippi River and in places by just the width of a street, Minneapolis and St. Paul have lived together for over a century in a marriage of convenience. There's interdependence with little love. St. Paul is older, more staid, and, as many a first-time visitor has decided for himself, more a western outcropping of the urbane East. Minneapolis is newer, bigger, brasher, and more inclined to throw its weight around.

When it became obvious that major league sports were coming, the Twin Cities girded for the fight in a manner as predictable to the home folks as it was baffling to outsiders. Clearly the area would attract just one team, but each city laid a trap — built a stadium, that is — anyway. St. Paul constructed one in St. Paul, thoughtfully convenient to Minneapolis. Minneapolis had built a stadium for a minor league team

A full moon picks out a solitary sailboat on Lake Harriet in Minneapolis.

11

earlier, but did it with expansion in mind. The site Minneapolis had selected was in suburban Bloomington, handy enough to St. Paul, but even handier to Minneapolis, to the nearby Twin Cities airport, and to four-lane highways.

The Twins and the Vikings chose Bloomington. (So, later, did the hockey North Stars.) This raised another problem. Professional teams play *somewhere* — the Detroit Tigers in Detroit, the Chicago Cubs in Chicago. But here were teams named not for a city but for a state. It had been a smart move to bid for broad fan support and to dampen intercity rivalry. But both cities had been anticipating the national publicity the teams would attract. To describe the games as being played in Bloomington would please no one except that suddenly pulsating suburb. Finally, after prolonged negotiations, and amid catcalls from the national press, it was agreed that for half the year the Minnesota Whatevers would play their games in a composite city called Minneapolis-St. Paul, and the other half in St. Paul-Minneapolis. There was a tendency for writers and television announcers to slip and say Minneapolis anyway, a fact which probably contributed, after a decade of such erosion, to the now general use of the Bloomington dateline that might well have been used in the first place.

During this characteristic squabble, the Twin Cities turned out to be innovators in an area social scientists might find fertile. This was the first instance of a major league sports team's being named for a state rather than a city. In its wake, as urban sprawl continues, we now have such baseball teams as the Texas Rangers with a constituency in both Dallas and Fort Worth, and the California Angels who play in a stadium at Anaheim, as well as the Golden State Warriors, whose National Basketball Association pennant flutters over San Francisco.

For all these intramural frictions, however, Minnesota is undeniably one state, bigger, colder, wetter, and more diversified than most of the other forty-nine by any yardstick. Though the home of billion-dollar businesses, Minnesota still draws almost half of its wealth from the soil. Its farms and villages make pictures which stir vague discontents in city people. It is so laced with lakes that a definitive count of their number is hard to make. Recent tallies have produced two to five thousand more than the ten thousand lakes celebrated on automobile license plates.

Minnesota's water is so abundant that it covers one-twentieth of the state's surface, a ratio which has long led the state to proclaim itself no. 1 in terms of inland waters. Recent federal figures have pulled the plug on the "most watery" boast. The 1970 census awarded the title to newcomer Alaska, with nearly twenty thousand square miles of surface water, four times Minnesota's. Even worse, from the point of view of state loyalists, the same count put Texas no. 2, with about four hundred more square miles of water than Minnesota.

In an unlikely debate on these honors, Minnesota might point out that the borders of both Alaska and Texas are washed by oceans, but Minnesota is tucked away in the center of the continent, about as far from salt water as a state can get. Yet Minnesota waters, split by a three-way continental divide within its borders, reach the Gulf of Mexico via Minnesota's own river, the Mississippi, find the Atlantic Ocean via Lake Superior and the Great Lakes-St. Lawrence system, and run toward the Arctic Ocean via the Red River of the North.

When in 1858 Minnesota became the thirty-second state, the Mississippi and Red rivers plus Lake Superior made the map makers' job easier. Together with a string of sparkling wilderness lakes on the Canadian border and the St. Croix River to the east, these waterways form the boundaries of more than half the state and give it the somewhat up-ended rectangular look it bears on the map.

To call Minnesota one big city surrounded by countryside is correct in one sense, misleading in another. There's also southern Minnesota and northern Minnesota. Southern Minnesota is dairy, grain, and cattle farms, with bigger towns and more people. Northern Minnesota is lakes and trees and rushing streams and rocky outcrops rising above the treetops. The towns are smaller and farther apart, but it's the vacation heart of Minnesota for visitors and residents alike. Northern Minnesota shelters two national forests, a wilderness string of waterways open only to canoes, and a newly authorized national park.

The northeastern tip of this part of the state is called the Arrowhead, which suggests both its shape on the map and the Indians who once had the place to themselves. The Arrowhead is outlined on the south by the shore of Lake Superior, the biggest, and still least polluted of the Great Lakes, and on the north by a string of lakes and streams along the Canadian border,

The cities of Minneapolis and St. Paul are not as different as night and day— except in these pictures. Above, the Minneapolis skyline. Below, the city center of St. Paul, skirted by a loop of the Mississippi River.

Wildlife is not unknown in the Twin Cities.
Above, a family of Canada geese on
Lake of the Isles. Below, a wild fawn snuggles near
a gravestone in a Minneapolis cemetery.

once the water highway of French voyageurs trading for furs with the Indians. In this area also lies the mightiest of Minnesota's three iron ore ranges, the giant Mesabi. And at the bottom corner of the Arrowhead, at the head of Lake Superior, sprawls the seaport of Duluth, whose ore and grain shipments make it, together with its twin port of Superior, Wisconsin, across the bay, the nation's second-busiest port.

Not quite all of northern Minnesota is rugged lake and forest country. Along its western fringe, on the North Dakota border, this landscape gradually gives way to the Red River Valley, the state's most fertile farm belt. The term "valley" is misleading. Actually it is the bed of an ancient glacial lake, flat as a Midwestern accent and so deep in rich black dirt that it has been a land of plenty for farmers from the state's earliest settlement.

Northern Minnesota is also the one place where you can wade across the Mississippi River without getting your feet wet — if you don't slip on the stones over which the infant stream gurgles as it leaves its source in pine-fringed Lake Itasca. The parent lake, by the way, was named for its offspring in a bit of pedantic whimsey. The Mississippi hooks its way through much of northern Minnesota before turning southward, and early explorers had great difficulty in determining where it began. In 1832 writer-explorer Henry Schoolcraft succeeded in tracking the river to its true source, or head. Taking the Latin words for truth and head, *veritas* and *caput,* he then lopped off the first and last syllables — ergo, Itasca.

In contrast to the cooler, piney areas of the north, southern Minnesota has what seems to me a kind of identity problem. It has lakes many states would envy, but most lack the aesthetic and recreational appeal of those up north. In the very southeast corner, the one section of Minnesota not shaped by glaciers, there are spectacular valleys and gentle streams and bluffs overlooking the Mississippi, as the now broad stream heads south. But elsewhere, southern Minnesota is mostly rolling prairie. It too is a country of productive farms. Besides small grains, dairy products, and meat animals, southern Minnesota grows corn, peas, and other vegetables to keep its canneries and quick-freeze plants busy during the harvest season.

This is a land of many small towns originally built to serve the surrounding farms when horse and wagon, or the occasional train, was the only way to get to town.

As the automobile left these towns with a diminished mission, some hung on in a kind of municipal dotage, some found ways to grow instead of die, and some discovered, or were blessed with, new ways to prosperity.

The best and best-known example is Rochester, a town with enough doctors for a city ten times its size. Rochester is the home of the Mayo Clinic, born of a country doctor's practice, whose medical skills draw patients from all parts of the United States and many countries overseas. Rochester was one of Minnesota's fastest-growing towns in the 1960s, its development given an assist by a vast new International Business Machines plant. A projection by the Upper Midwest Council (UMC) sees Rochester with 100,000 people by 1985, compared with 66,000 in 1970.

People whose names would make news in many countries are routine Mayo patients, in part, I suspect, because Rochester is remote from the vigilant eye of the competitive press in larger centers. The clinic makes a point of respecting a patient's privacy. A spokesman once told me, "We are a group of doctors engaged in the private practice of medicine, and we respect the doctor-patient relationship." News inquiries about prominent patients are often referred to an accompanying relative. The clinic takes no initiative in these matters. For example, the public did not know until after Ernest Hemingway took his life at his Idaho home that he had, shortly before, been a depressed and despairing patient at Mayo for weeks.

No matter how Minnesota can be subdivided in the mind, it remains one state. Its name, derived from the Sioux language, means clear water, or sky-blue water, or even cloudy water, depending on which authority one consults. It could be argued, in these days of belated concern over water pollution, that the various translations constitute a kind of prophecy of the white man's ways with the blessings of nature.

Certainly the state's waterways were cleaner in the seventeenth century when the first white invaders, French explorers and fur traders, saw them. Later came the English, and missionaries of both countries. Yankee lumbermen followed the fur traders, and settlers attracted by inexpensive and fertile farm land followed both. Germans, Swedes, and Norwegians, flowing in on the first great tide of immigrants, created the state's basic ethnic stock.

A map of Minnesota today traces not only its earliest

The Falls of Minnehaha in Minneapolis were celebrated by the poet Longfellow in his Song of Hiawatha, *although he never saw them. A statue of the legendary lovers, Hiawatha and Minnehaha, stands just above the falls. During dry spells the falls "laugh and dance, and leap into the valley" only when the city pumps water into Minnehaha Creek from a nearby lake.*

Above, water vapor over the Mississippi River in Minneapolis on a December morning. Below, pedestrians can escape the cold by a system of enclosed walkways which link an increasing number of downtown buildings.

highways — the lakes and streams — but mirrors, in many of its melodious place names, its French and Indian past and more recent infusions as well. Some of the names are logical enough, but some give the curious traveler pause.

Who would not wonder, seeing for the first time a southwestern Minnesota lake called *Lac qui Parle?* Indians called it, in the Sioux tongue, "Lake which Speaks." An unknown Frenchman found the name appropriate and stuck with it, in his language. *Lac qui Parle* it is today. *How* it speaks is less clear. Indian spirits lamented there, or waves splashed on the rocks in a certain kind of melody, or the winter ice sheath made its own sounds. Or maybe all of them.

There's no such doubt about *Pomme de Terre,* lake and river also in southwestern Minnesota. Except that the "apple of the earth" was actually a kind of turnip eaten by the Indians.

The map retains some Indian lake names, and Lake Winnebagoshish in northern Minnesota suggests why. The original Ojibway name means "miserable dirty wretched water," even more mouth-filling in translation than in the original and, to sportsmen who find it a good fishing lake, not quite fair. Lake Minnewaska, in central Minnesota, offers no such problems. Its name derives from two Sioux words meaning "good water." Other Ojibway names on the land are Mahnomen ("wild rice"), Menahga ("blueberry"), and Watab ("tamarack roots"). Sioux chiefs lent their names to the towns of Wabasha, Red Wing, Shakopee, and Sleepy Eye.

The Indian and French names survive chiefly among Minnesota's waterways. Town names are another matter. The early settlers who decided such things tended to honor developers, promoters, pioneers, and, often, their former homes in the old country.

National patterns are observable here. Yankee immigrants, with ancestral ties to the British Isles, seem to have raised a disproportionately large voice in naming communities — Cambridge, Dorset, Dover, Kensington, Kent, Manchester, and Lancaster, among others. Scandinavian settlers chose names like New Sweden, Oslo, and Upsala. Central Europe echoes on the map with names like Belgrade, Cologne, Danube, Hamburg, New Germany, New Munich, New Ulm, and New Prague. (New Germany became Motordale for a time during the anti-German feeling of World War I.)

There were other derivations. Historians disagree on whether Montevideo was named for the view it afforded

Horses gaze at cyclists pedaling down a quiet road near the Twin Cities.

Not far from the public beaches of Lake Harriet in Minneapolis,
this young couple found a secluded perch over the water.

Pawn shops and ten-cent beer (right)
marked the skid row of Minneapolis's lower loop
before urban renewal began to
transform the area in the 1950s.

or for the capital of Uruguay. And the name of the state's largest city, Minneapolis, meaning city of water, is a hybrid coinage of Indian and Greek words.

Most of the state's communities took root, as towns do, along some interruption of transportation. Minneapolis and St. Paul were no exceptions. They grew up around two major breaks in the region's system of waterways — a junction and a waterfall. The junction was that of the Mississippi River and its tributary to the west, the Minnesota. A high bluff commanded the junction, and in 1817 the site caught the eye of United States army officers looking over an area in which Indians would continue to be uncertain neighbors for another half century. Fort Snelling, the major army outpost on the upper Mississippi, was begun three years later.

The waterfall — the Falls of St. Anthony — lay just upstream on the Mississippi. These falls, long since harnessed by dams and locks, were named for his patron saint by the explorer-priest Father Louis Hennepin, who first saw them in 1680. The falls marked the end of the run for the steamboats that soon bore the heaviest burden of supplying the new territory. St. Paul, a few miles downstream and just across the river from Fort Snelling, served as the head of navigation and jumping-off point for settlers bound for the north and west. It became first the territorial and later the state capital.

By 1821 the troops building Fort Snelling had constructed a sawmill and stone gristmill at the falls to supply the garrison with lumber and flour. The village of St. Anthony grew up around the cataract's ample supply of water power. Years later St. Anthony was absorbed into the rival village of Minneapolis, founded about 1847 on the opposite bank of the Mississippi. St. Paul, meanwhile, had prospered as the major head of river navigation and a logical landing place for the politically ambitious.

In a century and a half the Twin Cities have grown into a metropolitan area of nearly two million people. The flour milling, lumbering, and river and rail transportation which spurred their growth have yielded in importance to a sophisticated electronics industry, international food conglomerates, varied manufacturing, and the other services and amenities that go with an urban center.

What surprises a first-time visitor — particularly one arriving in the summer — is the Twin Cities' blend of metropolitan hustle and fresh-water charm, a combina-

*Rural people know hard times, too. This couple near Cass Lake
in northern Minnesota supported a family of ten on seasonal and part-time earnings,
qualifying for maximum help under the federal food stamp plan.*

An elderly woman, room-bound by illness,
sits alone among her possessions.

tion that is rare in contemporary America. In other words, much of the Twin Cities area is green space, uncluttered and attractive. A visitor knows Minnesota has an abundance of lakes, but he probably doesn't realize that nearly a thousand of them can be found in the seven-county metropolitan area.

From their office windows workers in many Twin Cities towers can see sailboats and canoes making their leisurely way on blue water. Power boats are outlawed on the urban lakes, though the rules are waived for something splashy like a national water-skiing contest. The only real noisemakers are the swimmers and sunbathers who jam the public beaches on hot summer afternoons. Other lake users tend to be a quieter bunch — walkers, joggers, and fishermen who line the shores or drop their lines from jutting docks built especially for their use.

Twin Citians see nothing incongruous about a barefoot boy waiting at a bus stop, rod in one hand and string of fish in the other, or a housewife strolling across the road from her house to do a little evening casting from the shore without bothering to remove her apron.

"Tell me," asked a friend from New York viewing these activities for the first time on a summer afternoon, "does our company *pay* you to work here?"

Many of the rural towns in Minnesota can duplicate the trees and green grass and the inviting water of the Twin Cities. (The water, in fact, will probably be more inviting; for all their beauty, the urban lakes are heavily used, and show it.) And the rural communities can offer such attractions without the noise, the confusion, and the traffic jams of the cities. Since World War II Minnesotans, like other Americans, have increasingly tried to enjoy country pleasures without giving up a well-paying job or the cultural stimulation of the city center by commuting from outlying areas. During the 1960s, according to the Upper Midwest Council, only two metropolitan areas in the United States larger than the Twin Cities were growing at a faster rate. (They were Washington, D.C., and Houston, both nourished by heavy federal spending.) The result, typically, has been urban sprawl, hopscotching development, and overstrained public services. Since 1967 an agency known as the Metropolitan Council has wrestled with the social and physical problems created by the area's rapid development.

This expansionary trend rides the automobile culture and its concomitant, the high-speed multi-lane highway. The auto has, in effect, decentralized what the river and the railroad once centralized. People formerly had to live closer to their jobs, and the jobs had to be where water and rail transportation dictated. Witness the giant grain elevators and heavy industry that followed the routes of the Mississippi and the railroad network in the Twin Cities, and the urban cores which grew up close by. Now one can work in a city skyscraper or factory and drive up to fifty or sixty miles twice a day to do it.

During the 1960s the movement of people was both concentrated in and dispersed throughout the Twin Cities region. While the city centers lost population, the suburbs became the fastest-growing communities in Minnesota. Growth projections for the next ten years show this trend intensifying and spreading. A typical example is Forest Lake, a twenty-minute drive north of St. Paul. This pleasant town jumped 67 percent in population during the 1960s, and projections point to a bigger surge that by 1985 will double its size, from 8,500 to 17,000 people. Projections for other communities within an hour's drive of the Twin Cities are similar.

There are some exceptions to this pattern. St. Cloud and Mankato, slightly beyond the normal commuting distance to the Twin Cities, have grown rapidly, in part because they are becoming regional, as opposed to local, service centers. Marshall and Morris, well outside the Twin Cities zone of influence, have grown rapidly as a result of educational expansion. And Alexandria and Bemidji, the latter still farther outstate, have expanded partly because of what is called the amenity factor — meaning they are especially nice places to live in.

Overall, however, recent census figures measure the decline of rural areas. During the 1960s, Minnesota's population increased by 11.5 percent, lagging slightly behind the national average of 13.3 percent. As noted, this growth was concentrated chiefly in the Twin Cities. Meanwhile, of about one hundred and thirty outstate towns with more than 2,000 people, forty-one grew at less than the national rate and thirty stood still or, in most cases, actually lost people. Nearly half of Minnesota's counties had population losses. Fewer farmers were managing bigger farms.

In the words of the UMC: "The rural population has become more affluent, more mobile, and more selective in the procurement of goods and services. As a result, the small service centers are less and less competitive with the large centers in providing goods and

A youthful model inspires mixed reactions at a Minneapolis fashion show.

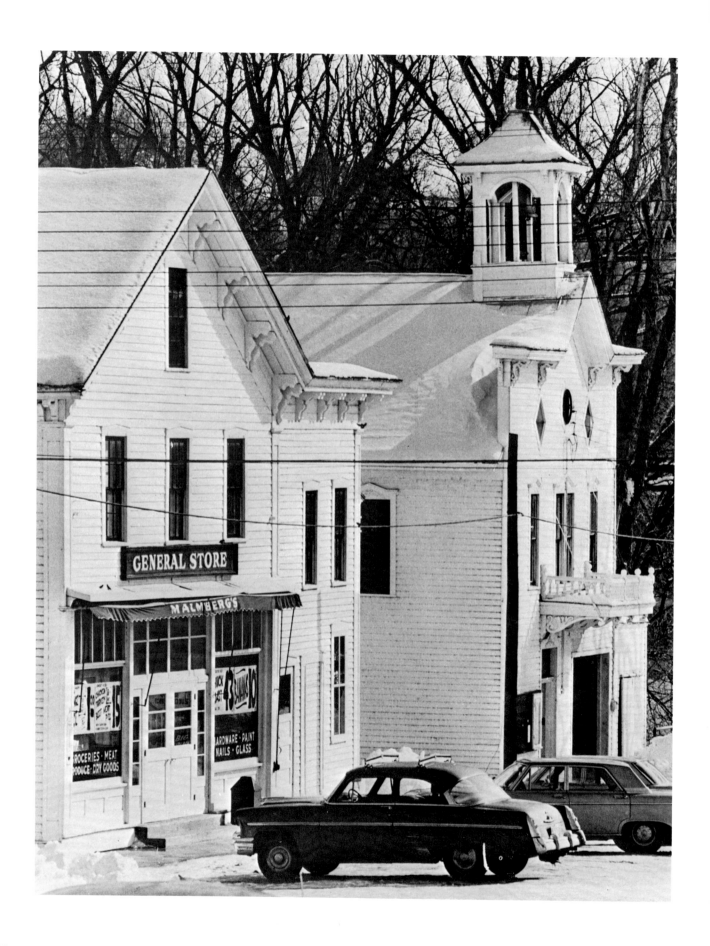

A boy and his dog on the lower St. Croix River, at the Minnesota-Wisconsin border. The St. Croix is one of the first "semi-developed" rivers to be managed jointly by state and federal governments. This area saw early growth. Marine on St. Croix (facing page) was the site of Minnesota's first lumber mill, built in 1839. The village today retains a New England flavor imparted by its Yankee founders.

services. There has been a gradual consolidation of services and population in the larger centers."

Traditionally, small towns have been more important socially and economically in the Midwest than in other parts of the nation, and their decline is viewed with anxiety by many people. Yet, except for the tiniest clusters of gas station, general store, grain elevator, and post office, their plight may not be all that desperate. They came to life in the days when a farmer needed to be within horse-and-wagon distance of a trading center. Their isolation was not only geographical, but also cultural and social.

A generation or two ago it was easier to find in small communities the sort of smug isolation pictured so graphically by Sinclair Lewis in his novel *Main Street.* Lewis's own hometown of Sauk Centre in central Minnesota was, despite pro forma denials, the model for his Gopher Prairie, a shabby, dull, complacent community, standing "unprotected and unprotecting," with "no dignity in it nor any hope of greatness."

Small communities today — like big ones, by the way — tend to be inward-looking. But their isolation is not what it once was. The mass media of radio, television, and quickly delivered newspapers rapidly diffuse facts, customs, and opinions. In addition, the more aggressive and fortunate have seen manufacturing plants or branch offices move in to take advantage of cheaper land, lower taxes, and the small-town pattern of life.

A French Renaissance style house in St. Paul, built about 1870, was the residence of Alexander Ramsey—first territorial governor, later a U.S. senator and secretary of war.

F. Scott Fitzgerald once lived in this Victorian brownstone on St. Paul's fashionable Summit Avenue. Here he finished his first novel, This Side of Paradise, *in 1919.*

Other towns, through the mobility provided by automobiles and better highways, have developed into interdependent clusters, each town supplementing the others in certain services. The crowded, polluted, and crime-ridden cities make these small towns seem an increasingly attractive haven. As the energy crisis deepened in the 1970s, some observers saw in the small town hope for drastically cutting the energy drain and reducing air and water pollution at the same time.

The Minnesota of the future, then, may be one of bigger cities and regional centers, of fewer and smaller small towns, of fewer farmers and bigger, more industrialized farm units. What is not likely to change much is the geography and climate which nature bestowed upon the area.

Minnesota is a long state, north to south, extending more than four hundred miles from the Canadian border at the top to Iowa on the bottom. It is a land of extreme seasonal changes. Winters are cold, snowy, and often seem interminable. Summer is a pleasant interlude, the more prized because of its brevity. Spring and fall, when they behave themselves, are spicy and invigorating changes of pace.

Because Minnesota is so strung out, there's a perceptible overlap of seasons. In the generally short spring, for instance, it's possible to see lilacs in bloom one day in southern Minnesota, but the next day near the Canadian border find them still three weeks away from flowering. In the fall, when the nights turn cool and the trees take on deep shades of red, yellow, and copper, the situation is reversed. A traveler can enjoy the fall colors in the north several weeks before trees along the southern border lose their green.

Gardeners in the north country are challenged by a growing season of scarcely three months. Some beat the frosts of May or June by starting their outdoor plants in homemade greenhouses or sunny windows, and hurry their outdoor growth with extra care. Southern gardeners can count on nearly two additional frost-free months. Snow, like cold, drops more heavily on the north — the average fall ranges from more than seventy inches in some northern areas to twenty inches in the southeast. Minnesota's coldest reading, 59 below zero, was recorded in the north and its hottest, 114 above, in the southern part.

Motorists in some sections of Minnesota put snow tires on their cars with the same sense of resignation they feel as they bring overshoes and snow shovels up from the basement. Almost as essential as snow tires, for the north-country driver who wants to be sure his car will start in the morning, is a little electric heater that can be attached to a car's engine and plugged into an outlet during the night. Some northern Minnesota motels offer heater cords which can be hooked up to cars. The ensemble somehow suggests a row of horses tied to a hitching rail. In truly cold weather the only important status symbol in Minnesota is a car that will roar into life after standing overnight in subzero cold.

The winter cold also throws a thick blanket of ice over the lakes, but dedicated fishermen just chop holes in the ice and keep right on fishing. Minnesota's winters are not unique in the north country, yet they're harsh enough to complicate the state's image. During the coldest months businessmen who have occasion to talk by phone with colleagues in other parts of the country are accustomed to fielding solicitous inquiries about how they're managing to survive there on the edge of the Arctic Circle.

The occasional paralyzing blizzards of winter convey a sense of drama that outweighs their destructive power. News accounts tell of snowbound motorists rescued by tractor or snowmobile, knots of stranded tourists spending the night in a village church or school, or the farmwife in labor being airlifted to the hospital. Loss of life is usually low. But despite modern highways and snow-removal equipment, a severe blizzard may cripple an area for days until plows open the roads. Sometimes, during an extended period of heavy snow and wind, districts are isolated for weeks. This situation has on occasion provided a clue to the altered economic status of some of today's farmers. A reporter once phoned a farm family in an especially hard-hit area to see how they were getting along.

"Dad and mother came back from Arizona when they finally got the roads open the other day," the farmer reported cheerfully, "but then we got snowed in again. The folks just said to hell with it, and went back to Tucson for the rest of the winter." (Dad and mother made the first lap by snowmobile.)

On November 11, 1941, when radio and weather warnings were in their infancy, Minnesota's worst blizzard of record took fifty-nine lives. In a sudden, sullen shift of wind, it caught lightly clad hunters in their duck boats and unprepared motorists on the roads.

Among natural disasters in Minnesota, the tornadoes of summer have taken greater tolls, not just in property

Two women in Victorian dress complement the late nineteenth century architecture of a Lake Minnetonka house built by Charles Burwell in 1883 and recently restored.

Fort Snelling was established by the army in 1819 at the junction of the Mississippi and Minnesota rivers. The post is now being reconstructed by the Minnesota Historical Society.

This main street is losing out to modern transportation. Lawndale was born along a railway and a road in horse-and-wagon days. By the late 1960s only six people lived in the village.

Another main street is secure in history. Sauk Centre's native son Sinclair Lewis called his best-known novel Main Street. *Street signs (right) recall the writer.*

damage but in loss of life. The deadliest was the twister of 1886 that killed seventy-four people in the St. Cloud area. In 1965 a series of tornadoes that stabbed at Twin Cities suburbs killed fourteen. Minnesota's worst flood — that same year, incidentally — took twelve lives.

The Twin Cities image-makers are seldom pleased by the way the state's snow and cold make news, but their inhibitions do not worry the hardy dwellers in the state's far north. Among towns where the United States Weather Service takes temperature readings are the two northern communities of Bemidji and International Falls, the latter squarely on the Canadian border. It is common for one or the other to turn up the nation's coldest reading on a given day. When Bemidji is so honored, International Falls jealously suspects that the Bemidji reading might have been taken at an unprescribed hour that happened to be colder, and vice versa.

Contributing more than these, perhaps, to Minnesota's subarctic image has been television coverage of its team in the National Football League, the Vikings. A spokesman for the baseball Twins once told me he wished his team had adopted the name Vikings first. But the Twins usually finish their season before the snow flies, something the pro football schedule seldom permits.

The Viking name itself suggests rugged blood and air brisk enough to keep it circulating. And when network television depicts a home Viking game in which referees grab brooms to sweep for evidence of snow-covered yard markers, the image is not impaired. Nor was it diminished when the Los Angeles Rams, fresh from the orange groves and palm trees of southern California, arrived in Minnesota one December for a post-season playoff to find their practice field buried under a foot of new snow. When snow-blowers started prospecting for turf under the blanket of white, news photographs of the process nudged Minnesota, in the national mind, even nearer the North Pole.

The people who live and flourish in this climate of extremes reflect an ethnic background that is predominantly northern and central European. Besides Yankees of English, Scotch, and Irish extraction, the Minnesota mosaic was early composed of Germans, Scandinavians, Poles, and Finns. Dutch and Danes, especially skilled in dairy farming, came too, and later, as the iron mines of northern Minnesota offered jobs, there arrived more Finns, Poles, Slovenes, Italians, and in lesser numbers immigrants from other areas of south-central Europe. Though ethnic strains have thinned, in many areas national customs and the pioneer spirit are still cherished with persistence and affection.

The United States Census Bureau keeps a kind of record of national origins by asking about parental native languages, but its most reliable figures are based strictly on race. These show that an overwhelming majority of Minnesota's nearly four million people are white — nearly 98 percent. Blacks numbered about 35,000 in the 1970 census, and American Indians 23,-000. Other ethnic groups, chiefly Chinese, Japanese, and Filipino, totaled around 10,000. Most minorities cluster, not without racial tensions, in the Twin Cities. Here, concentrated in substandard residential areas, lives a third of the state's Indian population. The remainder are on scattered reservations.

Overall, the resulting population mix is one that puts a high value on education. Though Minnesota ranked only twentieth in average personal income among states in the early 1970s, it stood fifth in the amount per pupil spent on education. It was well above its population rank in the number of public and private colleges it supported and could claim one of the nation's lowest rates of draft rejections for mental deficiencies. Whatever may be said about the state's tax climate (a subject so complicated it produces as many answers as there are researchers working on it), manufacturers looking for opportunities in Minnesota can count on one of the nation's best-educated and most stable work forces. In the cities labor tends to be heavily unionized, but one motive for plant expansion in small towns is availability of a labor force, including part-time farmers and their families, that is less costly than its counterpart in the cities.

This blend of people has created a dynamic political structure that, like the social climate, is a sometimes puzzling mixture of conservatism and liberalism. Third-party movements, for instance, have enjoyed far more than normal success. The official name of the Democratic party has been the Democratic-Farmer-Labor party (DFL) since 1944, when traditional Democrats fused with the liberal Farmer-Labor party which arose as a strong third force in Minnesota politics after World War I. As the historian Carl H. Chrislock points out, it was not until a decade after the 1944 merger that Minnesota first began to operate under a flourishing two-party system. Political observers give the state's voters high marks for their keen awareness of social and political problems and for their independent spirit. The state has contributed to the national scene such diverse figures as Senator and Vice-President Hubert Humphrey, Senator and 1968 presidential candidate Eugene McCarthy, and Chief Justice Warren Burger and Justice Harry Blackmun of the United States Supreme Court.

Conclusions about a state's character invite debate on a touchy subject, that variously defined commodity called quality of life. In 1967 a midwestern research institute ranked Minnesota second, behind only California, among the fifty states in quality of life. The criteria included education, economic status, health and welfare, and agriculture. In 1973 the same institute dropped Minnesota from second to thirteenth place. "Incredible!" "Idiotic!" cried officials paid to keep the state's public image shining. "The differences between Minnesota and any other high-ranking state are not significant," hastily explained an institute spokesman.

Meanwhile, a Washington, D.C., research institute measured the Twin Cities and seventeen other metropolitan areas in terms of fourteen specific social indicators. In this case, the bench marks included citizen participation in public affairs, income, quality of air, health, and similar factors. Though the Washington institute offered no cumulative score, a Minneapolis civic group totaled the ratings and concluded that the Twin Cities, in the aggregate, came in first — by a wide margin. This time there was no recorded outcry. □

The one-room rural school is disappearing.
This schoolhouse near Maple Plain, among
the last, was closed in 1967. At left, a student.
Facing page: A school bus from Grand
Marais makes its daily 120-mile run up and
back the Gunflint Trail in the
Arrowhead country.

The chapel designed by architect Marcel Breuer dominates the campus of St. John's University, the offshoot of a Benedictine abbey founded in central Minnesota in 1856.

The fine German-style brickwork of the New Ulm post office reflects the city's ethnic heritage. German is still heard on the streets, polka music on local radio.

Every July people gather at the Bramble Church, a small Russian Orthodox church near Togo in northern Minnesota, to celebrate the festival of Tikvin. Abandoned for some forty years, the building was restored in the 1960s. Worshipers come from many miles for the annual celebration.

A country church and cemetery near Echo, a little community in southwestern Minnesota settled by Norwegians.

Many Minnesotans keep fresh the customs and traditions of their European origins. Right, a suburban St. Paul girl, too little to join the fun, watches her elders at a German polka festival. Below, costumed youngsters join a flag parade on Norwegian Independence Day (Syttende Mai) at Minnehaha Park in Minneapolis.

Svenskarnas Dag—Swedish Independence Day—in Minneapolis.

The kolacky is a fruit-filled Czech pastry.
Lots of Czech (originally, Bohemian) immigrants settled around Montgomery,
in southern Minnesota. Montgomery has a Kolacky day,
complete with attractive girls.

Right, "Just say I'm a University student,"
a girl on Minneapolis's Nicollet Mall
told the photographer.

*Chippewa boys from Mille Lacs visited junior high school students
in Minneapolis during American Indian Week.*

*Elementary school children cautiously inspect each other during an
interschool exchange in Minneapolis.*

Large numbers of Irish came to Minnesota early in its statehood. Some settled in rural areas, but many were attracted to St. Paul. The city phone directory lists nearly two hundred O'Briens alone. St. Patrick's Day has become an unofficial, but uninhibited, civic holiday. A steadily growing feature is a downtown parade in which green is the color to wear and a leashed dog may march, too.

A student from Southwest State College at Marshall tells a legislative committee he opposes a tuition increase.

Ron Edwards, of the Minneapolis Human Relations Commission, speaks out against alleged police brutality.

In 1972 Indians massed in front of the Minneapolis city hall to protest what they called police brutality. The demonstration preceded a march on Washington called "Trail of Broken Treaties." Right, Clyde Bellecourt of Minneapolis, a leader of the American Indian Movement, took part in the 1973 occupation of Wounded Knee, South Dakota.

Young protesters move back from a spray of mace in the Cedar-Riverside area of Minneapolis near the university. The gathering began as a demonstration against urban renewal, but soon turned into a protest against the invasion of Cambodia and swept across the river into a major confrontation on the main university campus. Below, students on the main campus retreat before police.

*An Edina father welcomes home his son, released after four and a half years
in a North Vietnamese prisoner-of-war camp.*

Minnesota's best known modern political figure is Hubert H. Humphrey, who went from the Minneapolis mayor's office to the U.S. Senate and then served as vice-president under Lyndon B. Johnson. Humphrey's Minnesota home (in center of picture below) *is on Lake Waverly, half an hour's drive west of Minneapolis.*

The governor who occupied the domed state capitol in the early 1970s was Wendell Anderson. An Olympic hockey player during his student days at the university, Anderson still likes a game and is about to incur a tripping penalty (right, in dark uniform) in an alumni contest after his election in 1970. The athletic governor is a low-handicap golfer and also likes to fish.

43

*There are times when the topless sports car and Minnesota weather
are not made for each other. One winter day the owner of this convertible left it
on a street and forgot to convert it. Then it snowed.*

A broom is not routine equipment for football referees.
One came in handy, however, when a two-inch snowfall obliterated yard markers
during a Vikings-Forty-Niners football game at Bloomington in December 1969.

Cold faces: A dogsled racer.

A Minneapolis fireman.

Minneapolis shoppers bundled up against the weather.

A pedestrian.

Night on a Minneapolis street.

Above, a rotary snowplow cuts a lane through ten-foot drifts blocking a country road in southwestern Minnesota. Below, in the central part of the state, a January sleet storm coated this fence, as well as power and phone lines, with half an inch of ice.

49

*Above, Lake Mille Lacs, two hours north of the Twin Cities, is a favorite
of walleye fishermen, but not on a stormy September day like this one.
Below, wind-driven waves lash the shore of Lake Superior near Grand Marais.*

The Minnesota River drains much of southern Minnesota and during the spring runoff sometimes floods part of it too. Above, volunteers pile sandbags on a levee at North Mankato in an effort to keep the river within its channel. Sometimes the levees don't hold.

Although Minnesota is not in the heart of the tornado country, twisters are fairly common during the warm months. Above, a funnel reaches down from a mass of dark clouds over Medicine Lake. Facing page: On the night of May 6, 1965, an unusual series of tornados struck at Twin Cities suburbs and nearby communities. Above, a woman stands before her demolished farmhouse near Norwood-Young America. Another tornado in the same series (below) destroyed houses in Spring Lake Park, north of Minneapolis. These storms killed fourteen persons, destroyed about $50 million worth of property.

*Weather moods. Above, lightning stabs the dark sky over Minneapolis.
Below, an unseasonable drop in temperature produced patches of fog over the
Minnesota River valley near Burnsville. After an August hot spell,
the mercury had plunged to a record-tying low of forty-four degrees.*

Right, rain and mist darken a tunnel of trees near Lake Minnetonka.

Nature begins to restore life after a forest fire. A tiny fern, known locally as the snakeberry, raises green leaves beside a fire-blackened stump.

A quiet country road skirts a farm near Winona. Southeastern Minnesota, a region of hills and deep valleys, is the only part of the state not shaped by glaciers.

Minnesota is the nation's chief producer of wild rice, which is actually an aquatic grass. In the natural beds on northern lakes, the traditional Indian method of harvesting is the only one permitted. One person paddles or poles while a partner gently flails the ripened stalks over the canoe, releasing kernels of rice into the bottom. Above, canoes move out to the Nett Lake beds, the state's largest. Facing page (clockwise from upper left): beating rice into a canoe; poling a canoe through a thick stand; parching the rice over an open fire; a rice-filled canoe.

  Farmers now augment the traditional harvest by planting rice in artificial paddies and gathering the crop by machine.

Left, like a ghost on mist-shrouded Lake Superior, the Greek freighter Trias *stands off the Apostle Islands. One of the last ships to leave Duluth-Superior before the winter freeze-up, the* Trias *awaits supplies of fuel and food.*

    Above, a stream of wheat pours into the hold of a freighter during a night loading at Duluth-Superior.

Above, the propeller of a freighter fights harbor ice in subzero cold as the
ship makes a belated December departure from the twin ports of Duluth-Superior.
Below, a tugboat tows a log raft assembled at Grand Marais to its destination,
a paper mill in Wisconsin. Rafting logs across Lake Superior
in this manner has recently been discontinued.

Casting a gear at the American Hoist and Derrick Company in St. Paul.
The foundry makes castings of up to ten tons.

Above, locks, bridges, and dam on the Mississippi near downtown Minneapolis. The graceful Stone Arch railroad bridge, dating from the nineteenth century, crosses diagonally in the foreground. Upstream, showing at low water, is the concrete apron that now covers St. Anthony Falls. Beyond is the Hennepin Avenue traffic bridge. Facing page: Top, dwarfing other buildings on the Minneapolis skyline is the fifty-one-story building of Investors Diversified Services. In the foreground, the Foshay Tower. Bottom, St. Paul's new $28 million Civic Center, completed in 1973. It can seat 16,500 spectators for hockey and up to 19,000 for other events.

Industry and recreation coexist on the Mississippi. Left, a tugboat maneuvers against a background of grain elevators in St. Paul. Below, members of a rowing crew take their shell out on the sun-flecked river. Facing page: Loaded coal barges, pushed by a powerful little tugboat, symbolize the steadily growing barge traffic on the upper Mississippi.

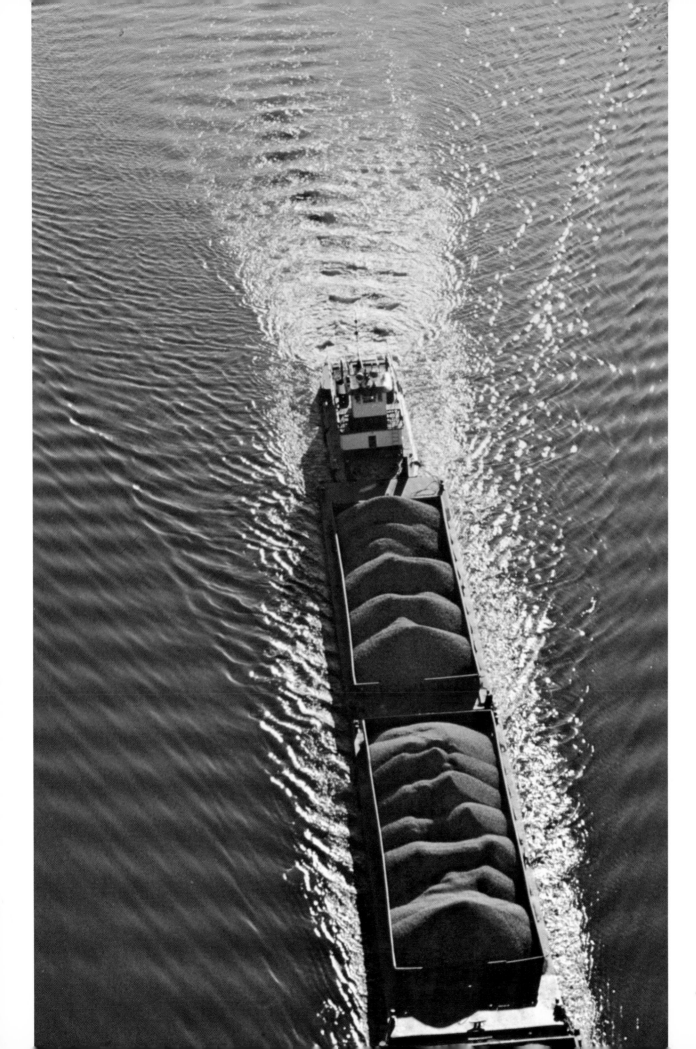

Facing page: Theatergoers line up along the gangplank of the University of Minnesota's showboat, the General John Newton, *shown here tied up at St. Paul. Right, a Minnesota artist with a greater reputation in Europe than at home is Charles Biederman of Red Wing, shown with some of his structurist reliefs. Below, one of the galleries at the Walker Art Center in Minneapolis. The city has two major art museums, the Walker more modern, the Institute of Arts more traditional, but both innovative in their programs.*

The nearly four million people who live in Minnesota own about four hundred thousand licensed boats. On a warm summer afternoon, hundreds of them can be seen at Lake Minnetonka, near Minneapolis. A view at Big Island, a favorite anchorage.

Fishing through the ice was once a sport for only the hardy. But development of the portable fish house—some with stoves, hole-to-hole carpeting, and other comforts— has transformed the sport. Fish houses on Gray's Bay, Lake Minnetonka.

*The sun shines on ice-coated trees after a sleet storm at **Zimmerman**.*

From Cornfields to Computers

*Window washers
at work on
the IDS building.*

From Cornfields to Computers

As a producer of wealth, Minnesota has one foot planted in the industrial East, the other in the agricultural Midwest. After more than a hundred years of statehood, the feet are very nearly the same size in terms of the dollar income they represent. In terms of geography, it's another matter. The southeastern corner of Minnesota lies within the northwest fringe of the industrialized East, or what has been called the American manufacturing belt. The rest of the state, except for isolated pockets here and there, draws its wealth chiefly from the land.

The Twin Cities and their suburbs are the center of manufacturing in Minnesota. Any charting of small-town industry shows a markedly greater concentration south and southeast of the Twin Cities than in the rest of the state. Waseca, a town of less than seven thousand people about fifty miles south of the Twin Cities, illustrates what can happen. Founded to serve the needs of surrounding farmers, Waseca now houses three large industries with national markets — a printing plant, a radio manufacturer, and a maker and supplier of sporting goods. Besides employing skilled professionals and technicians, these firms draw on surrounding towns and farms for their labor force. And, taken together, they conduct such a substantial mail-order business that Waseca's post office is the state's third busiest in terms of postal receipts.

Waseca, where presses and machines are next-door neighbors to cornfields, is a symbol of the balanced mix that agriculture and industry have become in Minnesota. It was midway in the twentieth century when manufac-turing first displaced farming as the major source of income. But food-processing income is included in manufacturing revenue, and agriculture remains vital to the Minnesota economy despite the expansion of industry.

The question of why what is made where — and sometimes when — is one that has long interested geographers and economists. Not uniquely, Minnesota's industry has tended to develop in two ways — by logic and by chance. What might be called the logic industries spring up where raw materials, transportation, and markets are available. The "chance" industries are not free of these factors, but are much less dependent on them than on the fact that an aggressive risk-taker got an idea, and decided to try it out right where he lived because he liked it there. This is something of an over-simplification and neglects such factors as the greater availability in some areas of a dependable and relatively inexpensive labor supply. But it's a usable key to the way Minnesota industry has grown.

Forestry, the state's first major business, today remains in third place behind agriculture and mining among industries which use natural resources. About one of every three acres in Minnesota is forested, despite heavy cuttings early in the state's history and vast clearing of tree stands for farming. Much of the white pine cut so prodigally by pioneer lumberjacks went straight into the building trades in Minnesota and in wood-hungry states farther south and east. Today the bulk of the lumber harvest is soft pulpwood which is fed into nearby mills at International Falls, Cloquet, and other sites with handy supplies of water to make paper and other wood-fiber products. Better grades of wood still go into the building industry, but in 1971 pulpwood accounted for almost seven-eighths of a $400 million forest harvest. Most of the pulpwood — aspen, poplar, and scrub pine — grows on cut-over or burned-over acreage, some of it planted, some natural growth.

Food processing was and is one of Minnesota's biggest industries. Visitors who want to see its birthplace can climb the stairs of the lookout at St. Anthony Falls, on the Mississippi River at the edge of downtown Minneapolis. Here the Pillsbury Company began grinding flour in 1869, as did an ancestor of present-day General Mills. For many years these mills and others along the waterfront earned Minneapolis the name of "Mill City." But convenience foods such as cake mixes and diversification into everything from restaurant chains to toy manufacturing long ago replaced milling as the mainstay of both firms. Both remain based in Minneapolis, however. Pillsbury sponsors a national baking contest, called the "Bake-off," which has become the Super Bowl of the kitchen.

General Mills, the larger of the two companies, has built itself a park-ringed home in suburban Golden Valley. As we drove past it one day, my small daughter identified it with a wave of her hand as "the place where the Lone Ranger gets all his money." Her generation too was aware of the firm's early and aggressive use of radio to sell its cereals. General Mills invented a cook named Betty Crocker, whose kitchens are a standard tour for convention wives visiting the Twin Cities.

Though recent demand for soybean products has given that crop a tremendous boost, Minnesota has long been, and still is, a grower of such traditional prairie state produce as wheat, oats, barley, and feed corn. But sweet corn, as well as peas and other vegetables for the table, are important crops too.

On a warm August afternoon, some years ago, as I was driving through the little town of Le Sueur, in the Minnesota River valley, an unusual sight caught my attention. Sitting on the curb outside a long, low building were perhaps thirty or forty white-uniformed men and women, laughing and talking like school children on recess. I stopped the car and asked what was going on.

"Corn pack," said a black-haired young man. "We're taking a break. Look out there."

In the direction he pointed I saw dozens of green, slatted wagons, each the size of a small truck and each overflowing with freshly picked corn, all lined up waiting to be unloaded. There, in what an advertising man later christened the "Valley of the Jolly Green Giant," I had wandered into the annual corn-picking and canning season. The Green Giant Company is one of many vegetable-canning and quick-freezing companies to establish plants near the truck gardens of southern Minnesota, but it is the only one to maintain corporate headquarters in the state.

Still another Minnesota food-based firm that looms large in the national and world economy is one of the least known. Cargill, Incorporated, bears the name of a Scotch family which began a grain-trading business in the Midwest in 1865 and which today remains largely family-owned in the face of an increasing tendency for large corporations to go public. Cargill is the largest privately held company in Minnesota and one of the largest in the United States. It was in the late 1960s that Cargill first revealed its annual sales had topped $2 billion. In 1973 that figure soared to more than $5 billion, an amount greatly swollen by unusually large foreign commodity sales, especially of wheat to Russia.

Cargill's operations, rooted in domestic and international grain trading, have expanded to include animal feeds, chemical products, and other commodities. Cargill owns its own fleet of ships and barges and has more than three hundred plants and offices in thirty-eight countries.

Quarries of granite and other building stone, dairies and meat processors, sugar beet and potato product factories — the list of smaller Minnesota industries related to the land and its products is a long one.

Minnesota has a well-developed transportation industry — international air service, extensive trucking facilities, railroads more important for freight than passengers these days, and a spreading network of highways. But in this jet age, where the new usually replaces the old, a way of transport that was vital to Minnesota in its youth — the Mississippi River — has made a spectacular comeback. By the turn of the twentieth century, the steamboats which once were Minnesota's main link to the world had given way to the railroad, and later to planes and trucks. In 1930 Congress authorized deepening the Upper Mississippi, along with a system of locks and dams, to encourage river traffic again. Flat-bottomed barges pushed by powerful little tugboats began to reappear on the river. Lovers of the old river

During high water the Mississippi plunges over a concrete apron built to prevent the erosion of St. Anthony Falls. Grain elevators stand on the right bank.

traditions took heart. So did the shippers of bulk goods adaptable to movement by barge.

Between 1935 and 1972 barge traffic into and out of the Twin Cities increased more than eightyfold. By 1972 the tonnage had topped 5,500,000 and was still growing, and more barges were being built to meet the growing need. At much the same pace of steamboats in a more leisurely era, grain, coal, and petroleum products slip slowly past the majestic bluffs of the Mississippi, bluffs that have recalled to more than one traveler the beauties of the Hudson or the Rhine.

Minnesota's other mighty waterway, Lake Superior, has long been vital to the state's economy. Iron ore, together with the grain grown by Minnesota and neighboring states, made shipping at the head of the Great Lakes a huge business. For many years the twin ports of Duluth and Superior ranked second to New York in total annual tonnage, despite being ice-locked much of the year. Since 1959 and the opening of the St. Lawrence Seaway, ocean-going ships have made world ports of Duluth and Superior. In the late 1960s Duluth-Superior shipped out nearly forty million tons by water and received about four and a half million tons. Other lake ports — Taconite Harbor, Two Harbors, Silver Bay, and Grand Marais — boosted the state's water transport tonnage by another twenty-five million tons, most of it iron ore and taconite.

Iron ore and taconite. Two products of the earth which have made deep imprints on the Minnesota economy. The former is a soft, reddish mineral found in long narrow beds among the woods and lakes of northern Minnesota. Huge fortunes were made — and some lost — on these iron ranges. Readily mined and easily shipped by way of the Great Lakes to steel mills, the state's rich deposits supplied for seventy years more than half of the nation's iron ore.

And taconite — that is another story.

An editor in the Iron Range town of Virginia picked a lump of rock from his desk and handed it to me. It was dark gray, irregular in shape, heavy, and hard. "That's a piece of taconite," he said. "The future of our region depends on it."

The year was 1951 and I, rock in hand, was puzzled. I had been getting my first look at the Mesabi iron range. I had seen the vast red holes in the earth and the steam shovels at the bottom dumping big bites of ore into railroad cars — all so far away they looked like toys. Long trains of the little ore cars chugged down the tracks toward Duluth and other lake ports. Red dust from the ore sifted onto roads, cars, and trees. Why, then, this unimpressive blackish rock?

"Our high-grade ores are becoming exhausted," said the editor. Some marginal mines, he went on, had already closed and others faced a similar fate. Before many years more, the ore would be gone. But taconite also contained iron ore, and there was an incredible amount of it in the earth near the soft ore beds — maybe as much as five billion tons. The trouble was that blast furnaces couldn't use taconite in unrefined form. Its ore content had to be extracted, concentrated, and processed before it could be shipped east to the mills.

This process, as the editor well knew, had already been perfected, largely by the late E. W. Davis and his colleagues at the University of Minnesota School of Mines. The end product, a round pellet about the size of a marble, would handle well in the blast furnaces. What remained was for the big steel companies to get into taconite production as the original ore industry phased out. To do this, they wanted to be assured of what they considered a nondiscriminatory tax climate. Although some taconite plants were opened before this assurance was forthcoming, in 1964 Minnesota adopted a constitutional amendment guaranteeing equality with other manufacturing, and the industry has been expanding rapidly since. In 1957 less than 10 percent of Minnesota's iron ore output was in taconite. By 1972 taconite accounted for nearly 70 percent of the state's ore production, and tonnage was growing steadily.

To the state's economy, and particularly that of northern Minnesota, the taconite industry has brought new life. But to those concerned with preservation of the environment, it has meant problems too. The most spectacular concerns Reserve Mining Company's plant on Lake Superior at Silver Bay, which went into operation in 1955. The process of turning raw taconite rock into concentrated pellets produces huge quantities of a residue called tailings. Reserve was granted permission to dump its tailings into Lake Superior, on the theory they would promptly settle to the bottom in the immediate vicinity and bother no one. But environmentalists charged that the tailings were polluting lake waters far from the plant's site, and litigation over the issue began in federal court in 1973. The suit promised to be an extended one and to be appealed to higher courts, whatever its outcome.

Other taconite plants in Minnesota are located in-

A section of the Mississippi River bank in north Minneapolis. Planners hope to reduce or eliminate such areas of industrial blight along the river.

Some boats are for work, some for play. A towboat pushing an empty barge on Lake Pepin, a widening of the Mississippi in southeastern Minnesota, cuts past a cluster of fishermen.

land, and dispose of their tailings in low-lying, usually swampy areas.

What of the "chance" industries, the foot-loose businesses unrelated to the soil or to natural resources that seemingly just happen to take root and flourish somewhere? Minnesota has these, too, among them a group of companies that have given the state an international reputation as a "brain industry" center. They make computers and other electronic equipment, and they are among the leaders in the industry.

Here, Honeywell is an anomaly. It was not a pioneer in the field but through acquisition has now become the nation's second largest computer manufacturer. Today an international industrial giant with annual sales of well over $2 billion, Honeywell grew from happenstance beginnings as a tiny enterprise in Minneapolis in 1883. That year an inventor developed a system for the auto-

matic control of house temperatures and hired six people to help him. From home controls, Honeywell expanded into industrial climate controls, guidance systems for defense and space exploration, and in 1970 into computers by buying General Electric's computer business. In 1972 control systems still accounted for one-fifth of Honeywell's world-wide sales, but computers and related information systems made up half of its total business.

To the extent that Minnesota can claim a share in the paternity of the fast-growing computer industry, that claim lies with other plants. Directly after World War II a group of Navy veterans — scientists and engineers all — got together in Minneapolis as Engineering Research Associates (ERA), Incorporated. Electronic data processing received a wartime boost from the armed forces, and these men envisioned the peacetime development of electronic storage, retrieval, processing, and manipulation of data — in a word, computers.

They succeeded, rapidly expanded in the Twin Cities, and in 1952 were acquired by Remington, Rand, Incorporated, which itself soon merged with the Sperry Corporation. In 1955 the ERA name disappeared with the establishment in St. Paul of the Remington Rand Univac Division of Sperry Rand. Univac (the name comes from ERA's first machine, the Universal Automatic Computer) retains its biggest operation in St. Paul, though corporate headquarters are in suburban Philadelphia.

Control Data, another major Minnesota computer firm, began in effect as a sort of spin-off from Univac.

Above, a dredge maintains the nine-foot channel on the Mississippi in Minneapolis. The channel, which has permitted barge traffic on the upper river since the 1930s, is increasingly popular with shippers and increasingly unpopular with environmentalists. Left, towboat and barge entering a lock at the Ford Dam. At this point the river divides Minneapolis, on the right, from St. Paul, on the left.

The Rainy River (above) *flows between Fort Frances, Ontario, on the left, and International Falls, Minnesota, on the right. The falls supply power for paper and wood-product mills on both sides of the river. Sophisticated machinery (below) is replacing the logger's ax and saw. This device, known as a "feller-buncher," grasps the tree, cuts it off near the bottom, shears the limbs, and stacks it.*

In 1959 Duluth and Superior, Wisconsin, became international ports.
Early in 1973 the first ship from the U.S.S.R. arrived. Sailors on the Zakarpayte
get a look at Duluth before their ship takes on a load of wheat.

Founded in 1957 by a group of Univac employees who left to start their own firm, Control Data was quickly and spectacularly successful, enriching in the process investors who had bought into its first stock offering at a dollar a share.

Minnesota is the home of another international industrial giant which seems neither a logic nor a chance industry, but has elements of both. It began in 1902 as an ill-fated mining venture on the North Shore of Lake Superior. The backers believed they had found a lode of corundum, a valuable abrasive used in making grinding wheels. They soon discovered their mineral was only a low-grade abrasive of no commercial value, and the infant firm nearly went under until it turned to manufacturing sandpaper at a plant in Duluth. A few years later the company was moved to St. Paul so that a major stockholder could keep a closer eye on it.

The firm is the Minnesota Mining and Manufacturing Company, often called 3M, and in 1972 it reported gross sales in forty countries of over $2 billion. For most of its career, 3M has put a premium on research, whether it seemed to focus on specific company goals or not, and has given its scientists and engineers leeway accordingly. Over the years 3M has found many things to make besides sandpaper. A major product with which the company has long been identified is Scotch tape. From its sprawling corporate headquarters east of St. Paul, 3M has expanded into magnetic tapes for the communications industry, tape recorders and other electronic devices, copying machines, adhesives, reflectorized signs and tapes, health care products, and photographic and printing equipment.

To close this look at Minnesota industry on a less cosmic note, it's been observed that the establishment of breweries has tended to follow the concentration of German-origin families. As in some other lines of work, the tendency among breweries has also been toward consolidation. The outstate breweries have been shutting down their vats, one by one, until the chief plants remain concentrated in the Twin Cities. Except for two. One can still sip a hometown brew in Cold Spring and New Ulm. Both towns have lots of Germans. □

Above, an irregular-shaped peninsula of taconite wastes dumped into Lake Superior
near the Reserve Mining Company's plant at Silver Bay. Charges that these
tailings were polluting Lake Superior grew into a major lawsuit in 1973.
Below, seven ore boats tied up for loading at Duluth. The ore, transported to the
docks in railroad cars, is tripped into bins and then released into the freighters.

This solitary commercial fisherman, photographed in 1959, represented a declining trade. Norwegian-born Helmer Aakvik worked his nets on Lake Superior the year round.

*Commercial fishermen on the Mississippi near Winona. The fish won't spoil;
the temperature was near zero when this picture was taken.*

*The face of a Control Data technician reflected by a stack of disc packs. Each disc
is a computer memory unit about the size of a phonograph record.*

Above, a Honeywell engineer sits at a computer console which regulates the temperature and humidity of fifteen Minneapolis buildings, indicated on the map. Developed in the early 1970s, the service has since been expanded to other cities. Facing page: The inside of a giant electric generator at Northern States Power Company's nuclear plant at Monticello. The reactors which furnish the power are elsewhere. This plant provides sufficient electricity to operate more than half a million homes. NSP has a second nuclear plant at Prairie Island, southeast of the Twin Cities.

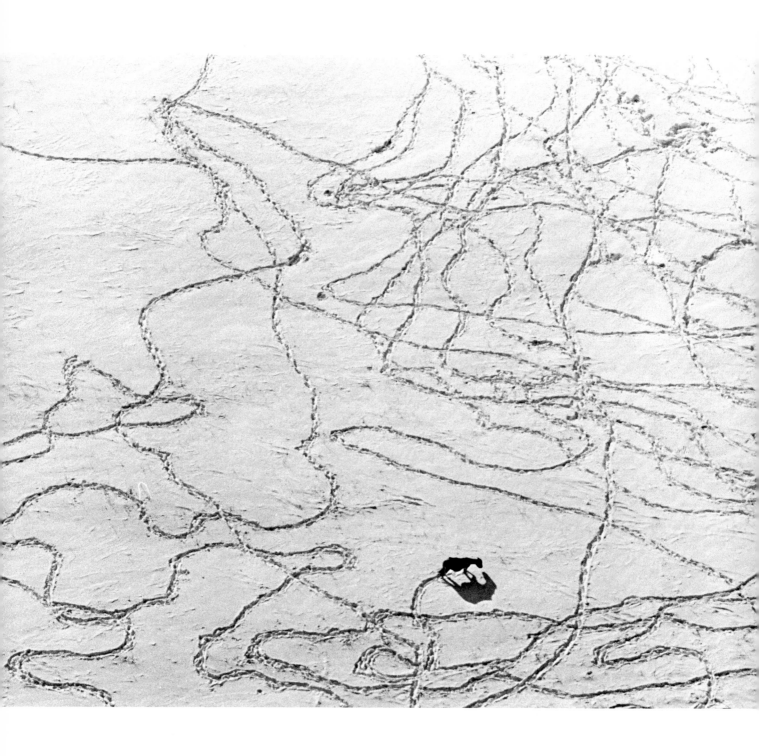

A horse, for reasons of his own, made this lacy pattern of tracks in fresh snow at a farm near Shakopee. Facing page: Top, vehicles and feet stamped out a snowy diary on a farmyard. Bottom, winter sometimes loses track of time. The proprietor of an open-air garden store in Minneapolis confronts a spring snowstorm.

Though a northern state, Minnesota produces good apples. Orchards (above) curve around a hillside near the prime apple-growing region of La Crescent. Below, a farmer cuts a field of oats on a Hennepin County farm.

From the family practice of a country doctor, the Mayo Clinic in Rochester (above) *has grown into an internationally known center of medical practice, research, and education. Below, a freshman medical student at the Mayo Medical School in Rochester stands in the courtyard of the clinic's diagnostic center. The school opened in 1972.*

93

Dr. William A. Nolen (above), *a busy general practitioner in Litchfield, has made a second career as an author. He has published two best-selling books and writes for magazines. There is a perennial shortage of doctors willing to practice in small towns. To help fill the gap, physicians' assistants are being trained to perform many services ordinarily left to doctors. Below, a PA examines a child at the Plainview Health Facility.*

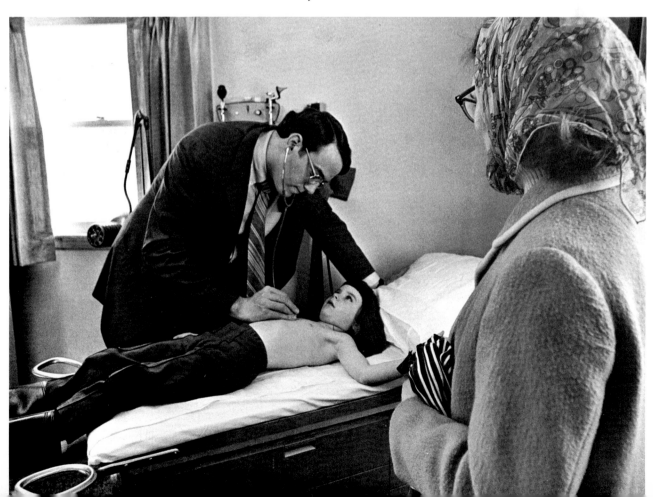

At the University of Minnesota Hospitals, a group of school children watch open-heart surgery, a technique university surgeons helped to develop. Below, a medical team performs an open-heart operation at Metropolitan Medical Center, Minneapolis.

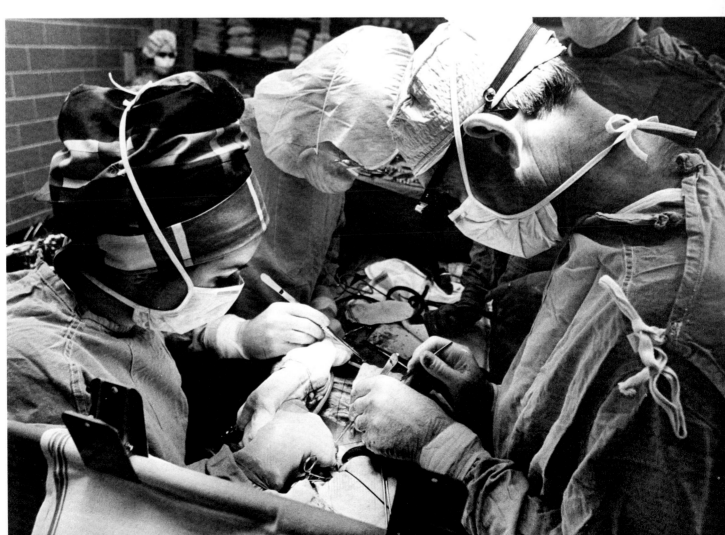

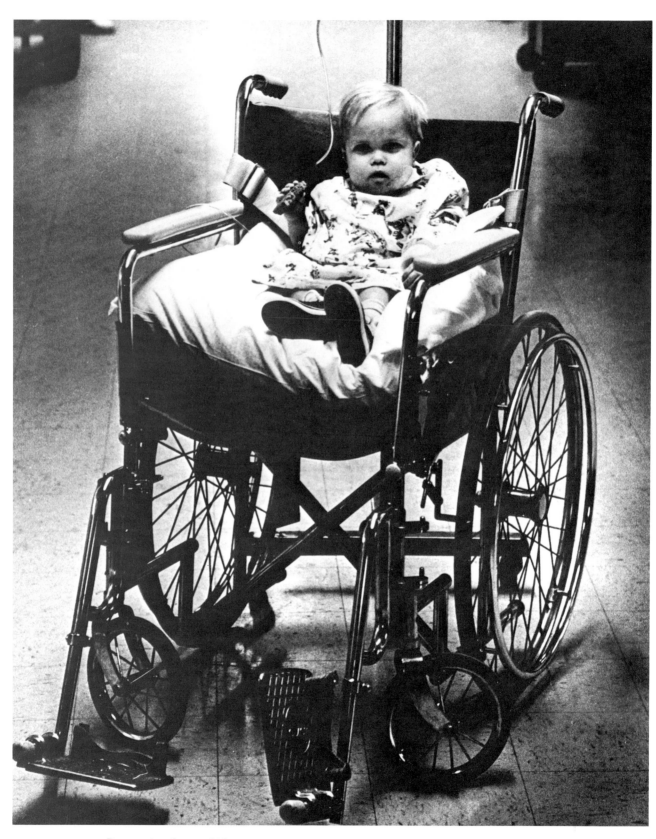

Recovering from a kidney-transplant operation, a two-year-old patient eats a snack at the University of Minnesota Hospitals.

Diversions and Recreations

A loon stretches his wings on a northern lake. The cry of the loon, Minnesota's state bird, has an unforgettable, haunting quality.

Diversions and Recreations

Minnesota is an agreeable state in which to play. Its pleasant summer climate, its lakes and streams, its forests and wilderness areas draw vacationers from hotter, drier regions. Yet Minnesotans too like to vacation in their own backyard. This clouds the picture somewhat when it comes to counting tourist dollars, an important part of the Minnesota economy.

What state economists call the "tourist-travel" dollar doubled in the 1960s, neared nine hundred million in 1972, and showed signs of reaching one billion before the energy crisis emerged. About half of that dollar, the state Department of Economic Development is careful to point out, appears to be coming not from outsiders but from Minnesotans. A study of the occupancy of state parks and resorts in the mid-sixties revealed that Minnesotans outnumbered, but by only a small margin, tourists from all other states combined in using these recreational facilities.

Apart from natural resources themselves, the enthusiasm of Minnesota residents for their own turf may be the most important single ingredient in the state's business health and vigor. The thesis does not lack for advocates. One of them is a friend of mine who publishes a daily newspaper in International Falls. Harry Davey moved to that small town on the Canadian border from the comparative warmth of southern Minnesota, even though he knew all about the rigorous border winters. I first stopped by his office in mid-afternoon of a pleasant June day. When I stated my business, he glanced at his office clock and suggested we could just as well confer while fishing for walleyed pike on Rainy Lake. The place on the lake where Harry kept his boat was a five-minute drive away. So we went fishing, and we talked a little business. We also caught a boatload of fish before we quit.

As we unloaded our catch in the cool, pine-scented twilight, Harry told me he had moved to International Falls not because he thought he'd make a lot of money, but because summer there had hooked him. In winter — well, you go for snowmobile rides and tell lies to wide-eyed southerners about how cold it gets.

Minnesota is so proud of its recreational resources it sometimes gets caught in its own superlatives. Harry and I were two of the million and a half fishermen who buy Minnesota licenses each year, some three hundred thousand of them coming from other states to do so. Minnesota champions have been known to claim this as a national record. Yet federal figures reveal Minnesota must yield to both California and Texas in this competition. The often-heard assertion that Minnesota has enough watercraft to give every resident a boat ride simultaneously yields to no such easy deflation. We do know that Minnesota licenses about four hundred thousand boats and canoes annually.

Without worrying the statistics more, it's safe to say that no one in Minnesota is more than a few minutes away from some kind of outdoor recreation. This is as literally true in the Twin Cities area as it is in the rest of the state. Fishing, swimming, and boating are all urban pastimes. On a warm Sunday when the breeze is fresh, two big lakes within a half hour's drive of the Twin Cities, Minnetonka and White Bear, are covered with sail and power boats, some of them based on the lakes, others hauled in for the day on trailers.

But to thousands of Twin Citians, the water is fresher and the fish more accommodating up north, in what is called the lake country. Each Friday afternoon in summer, good weather or bad, highways leading north from the cities are jammed with families heading to lake cottages they own or rent. "Up at the cabin" or "up at the lake" is all one needs to know about an absent neighbor. This is such a way of life in Minnesota that one out of every fourteen families in the state owns a part-time vacation house. Of the more than seventy-two thousand seasonal homes, five-sixths are owned by Minnesota residents. The trend runs so strong that in several northern Minnesota counties seasonal homes constitute almost half the total dwellings. In one county, Cass, they actually outnumber year-round houses.

(Southern Minnesota, it should be said, is by no means without lakes, but they are fewer and farther apart, and this region lacks the forests and other attractions that have made northern Minnesota prime resort country.)

To the year-round residents of the north, both city weekenders and longer staying vacationers represent money and, occasionally, annoyance. But many of the north-country natives live on or so close to the water that they can be fishing only a few minutes after locking their desks or leaving their homes. Thus they tend to be not only more philosophical about the weekend bulge of visitors, but more relaxed about their own work and play. "Closed — Gone Fishing" is a common sign on small-town shops when the annual season opens in May, but it is not unknown on pleasant days in the heart of summer.

Although lake fishing is the most common kind in Minnesota, stream fishing has its followers and its haunts. Most stream fishermen take trout with flyrods. The natural habitat of both are the fast-running rivers of the North Shore of Lake Superior and the gentler brooks of southeastern Minnesota, some of which flow through valleys of considerable beauty, flanked by hardwood forests and limestone ravines.

A Minnesota fishing scene that defies classification involves a tiny, silvery fish known as the smelt. Each spring this cold-water species leaves its Lake Superior home and pours into North Shore streams to spawn. This is the smelt run. When it begins in earnest, a remarkable rite of spring gets under way. Smelters descend on Duluth and the nearby shores by the thousands in cars, trucks, campers, anything on wheels. They come with dip nets, washtubs, barrels, pails. Often enough, too, they fortify themselves with beer and whiskey against the cool night air, for smelt make their upstream runs at night. Fires flickering on the beaches light up a kind of north country fiesta. There's also commercial smelting, but it's the amateurs who have the fun.

Logically enough, for an area well-endowed with outdoor resources, Minnesota has developed a park system worthy of a bigger state. Only seven states had more than Minnesota's ninety-eight state parks in 1970, though eighteen had more people. And to this Congress added in 1971 Voyageurs National Park, more than two hundred thousand acres along the Canadian border waters expected to be open by the late 1970s.

Skiing was imported to Minnesota by stubborn Scandinavian settlers when the state was young. Early equipment was clumsy, and skiing was mostly a deep-snow necessity, except for the nervy few who developed the sport of ski jumping. After World War II tows and lifts made skiing less laborious, snowmaking equipment improved, and Minnesotans took to the slopes with glee and abandon despite the fact that the state's gentle hills could by no stretch of the imagination be considered mountains. More and better lifts and runs were built, and such comforts as lodges, indoor swimming pools, game rooms, and saunas appeared. More recently cross-country skiing, with its simpler pleasures and less expensive equipment, has enjoyed a booming popularity.

Snowmobiles have become another way of enlivening the Minnesota winters, but they create more noise, and so do their detractors. Originally an unregulated curiosity, the snowmobile made a modest debut in Minnesota around 1960. Ten years later it had become a big business. By 1973 there were more than three hundred thousand licensed snowmobiles in the state and the total was growing. Minnesota manufacturers were building a third of the nation's supply.

As both a leading maker and user of snowmobiles, Minnesota has done some pioneer wrestling with the difficulties they create. Noise, especially at night, trespass, destruction of private property, and mounting accidents — all have contributed to the dilemma. The solution involved a compromise typical of Minnesotans' usually equable approach to social problems. On the one hand the machines were licensed and restricted in their running room, speed, and hours of operation, particularly in the metropolitan area. On the other hand the state began programs in safety education and developed some three thousand miles of open snowmobile trails on public and private land.

Fishing is convenient—and relaxing—in the Twin Cities. These anglers supervise their poles on the shore of Lake Harriet, in the heart of Minneapolis. City lakes yield panfish, pike, and other game fish.

Another outdoor sport that has bloomed with particular vigor in the Minnesota winter is the ancient Scottish game of curling. Curling may denote hairstyling in much of the country, but in a few of the northern-tier states, it means skidding a 42-pound stone down a long, narrow strip of ice toward a 6-foot target zone. Teammates try to guide the stone by strenuous sweeping with a broom before or behind it, depending on whether the stone's progress is to be speeded or slowed. Centuries old, curling long depended on natural ice. But, like hockey and figure skating, it has moved indoors onto artificial ice, a trend encouraging the social amenities with which curling has long been associated. Minnesota has named a state championship team annually since 1891, and curling is now an interscholastic sport.

In many states, the kind of hunting that Minnesota provides would make it that state's no. 1 outdoor sport. Though hunters can take white-tailed deer, moose, black bear, and a wide variety of game birds, fishermen outnumber hunters about five to one in terms of licenses issued. Third in fishing licenses, Minnesota ranks fourteenth among states in the sale of hunting licenses. Upland game — chiefly pheasants, partridge, and grouse — provides much popular sport, but hunters concentrate more on migratory waterfowl — ducks and geese.

The duck hunters, as well as many a conservationist who never fired a gun, argue passionately about the massive Minnesota wetlands drainage program. For many years potholes, shallow lakes, and other low-lying areas of southern and western Minnesota were systematically drained and the reclaimed land put under the plow. It tended to be fertile crop land. By 1960 one-fifth of the total land area of Minnesota had been drained for farm use. The gain in cash crops, conservationists argued, was made at the expense of wildlife, particularly waterfowl. The wetlands had provided nesting areas and habitat for the flocks of ducks that once blackened the prairie skies. The argument over land use is an enduring one. Drainage foes, who also blame the program for lower water tables, stream siltage, and more rapid water runoff in times of flood, have initiated schemes for wetland preservation.

Duck hunting (with what appears to be diminishing success these days), fishing, golf, skiing, tennis — these are participant sports, as opposed to what have come to be called spectator sports. The latter term is tinged with opprobrium on the ground that it's healthier to do it yourself than to watch someone else doing it. To be technical, though, if someone's watching, someone else is doing, and the number of Minnesotans — usually of school age — who compete against each other in football, basketball, hockey, and other team sports runs well into the thousands.

If the per game proportion of spectator to performer is given weight, perhaps the most truly spectator sports are provided by the professionals. Minnesota's major league teams in baseball, football, and hockey — all based, as we have seen, in the Twin Cities — draw crowds that keep them solvent, whatever their place in the league standings.

The same point can be made about cultural entertainment. It's a tiny community indeed that does not provide musical and dramatic outlets — usually school or church affiliated. But the proportion of consumer to producer, to use another industrial analogy, is again altered when one considers such popular organizations as the St. Paul and Duluth civic opera companies, the internationally famed Minnesota Orchestra, and the much younger but widely known Guthrie Theater.

Since Minnesota is known as an activist state (in its recreation as well as its politics), the Guthrie experience offers a useful footnote. When Sir Tyrone Guthrie and his colleagues put the regional repertory company together in Minneapolis in 1963, its professional competence cast a dark shadow — or so it was supposed — on amateur and other professional theater in the Twin Cities. Instead, the Guthrie proved a stimulus to smaller drama groups, some amateur, some professional, which have been innovative and often successful.

Sometimes the pace is set in unexpected places. Choral singing, drawing on the talents and tradition of German and Scandinavian immigrants, has always been a vital part of the musical tradition. But it was at a small college in a small town — St. Olaf in Northfield — where a capella singing was brought to a high degree of excellence by F. Melius Christiansen. The influence of the St. Olaf Choir and other college groups in the region has helped produce what some observers believe is the nation's finest choral tradition.

Attending a concert, watching a game, or more likely getting out and doing it themselves, Minnesotans find that the rhythm and pattern of their sharply changing seasons provide them with a generous variety of ways in which to enjoy themselves. To go mountain climbing, ocean surfing, or deep-sea fishing, Minnesota pleasure-seekers must, undeniably, travel. But not for much else.

According to river tradition, steamboats engage in a friendly race the first time they visit a city each year. When the Delta Queen, *last big riverboat to take passengers on long-range trips on the Mississippi, arrived in St. Paul, the only sternwheeler present to honor the tradition was the little* Jonathan Padelford. *Based in St. Paul, the* Padelford *carries tourists and parties on short summer excursions.*

Canoe-topped cars frame a summer street scene in Ely, just south of the Canadian border. Once a railhead for ore from the nearby Vermilion iron mines, Ely is best known today as a jumping-off point for canoe parties bound for wilderness areas to the north.

Framed by trees in autumn dress, a North Shore stream so tiny no one bothered to name it drops down a rocky shelf to join nearby Lake Superior.

*Maple and other broadleaf trees along the North Shore blaze with fall colors.
A few isolated pines in their midst remain green. Facing page: An abandoned windmill
that once pumped water for a northern Minnesota settler.*

A lone hiker plods through deep snow in the boundary waters country of the north. This stretch of shoreline, more open than most, will be part of Voyageurs National Park. The name derives from the French Canadian voyageurs, canoemen in the fur trade who once used the border lakes as a route between Lake Superior and the wilderness fur posts. Facing page: Kettle Falls, shown from the air, lies on the border waterway between Namekan and Rainy lakes. The flowing current keeps a channel open even in winter. This waterway, on the eastern tip of the Kabetogama peninsula, is also in Voyageurs National Park.

One of the boundary water area's best known guides, Bill Magie of Duluth, was still active at the age of seventy-two when these pictures were taken. Above, an early morning mist hovers over the lake as Magie stirs up the fire before cooking breakfast. Facing page: Top, canoe paddle in hand, Magie gazes at a waterfall in the narrows between Thomas and Fraser lakes. Bottom, Magie, in black-and-white plaid shirt, sits in front of a campfire with a group of fishermen.

Winter or summer, the Boundary Waters Canoe Area in the Superior National Forest attracts wilderness devotees. It lies along the Canadian border east of Voyageurs National Park. Motorized equipment is barred from all but a few designated routes in its million acres of lakes and streams. Above, snowshoers at the edge of an ice-locked lake. Facing page: The BWCA is busier in summer. A pair of canoers paddle toward the sunset on Nina Moose Lake.

Curtain Falls, between Crooked and Iron lakes in the boundary waters region. This falls was one of many barriers on the voyageurs' highway which required laborious portaging of canoes and their loads of furs or trade goods.

Top, a cloud-flanked setting sun silhouettes campers and their tents on Crooked Lake, in the boundary waters. Below, a canoe party prepares to leave the Professor Island campsite on Lac La Croix, boundary waters.

Painted Rock on Lac La Croix is faced with Indian pictographs which continue to baffle scholarly investigators. The figures of moose are identifiable in the crude drawings which have withstood the erosion of centuries. Little is known about which Indian tribes painted them, or how long ago, or what materials and techniques were used.

A Grand Marais couple, Mr. and Mrs. Ben Gallagher, built this summer home
on an island in Magnetic Lake, near the end of the Gunflint Trail.
The U.S.-Canadian border runs ten feet from the front porch. Below, canoes
on Nina Moose Lake, farther west in the Boundary Waters Canoe Area.

The temperature stood at forty-nine degrees below zero and the wind chill factor
was a minus seventy-five degrees when the International Dogsled Races were run
at Ely. Above, vapor rises from idling automobiles behind the starting area.
Below, a racer with frosted face mask guides his dog team through woods.
Facing page: One racer wrapped his face in a scarf against numbing cold.

Snowmobile tracks from the air.

Ice-coated branches spread over a stream on the Gunflint Trail in the Arrowhead country.

Chiefly a recreational vehicle, the snowmobile is an increasingly popular way of getting around during snowy winters. Above, snowmobiles parked in front of a rural church near St. Paul. Facing page: Boy Scouts from Thief River Falls set out by snowmobile for an overnight camping trip.

Winter sports are encouraged by the Minneapolis Park Board's recreation program, and nowhere is the scene livelier than at Wirth Park. National ski jumping champions have gotten their start at Wirth. Above, a youngster discovers that snowshoes are big and tough to manage. Facing page: Two young cross-country skiers take to one of the Wirth trails.

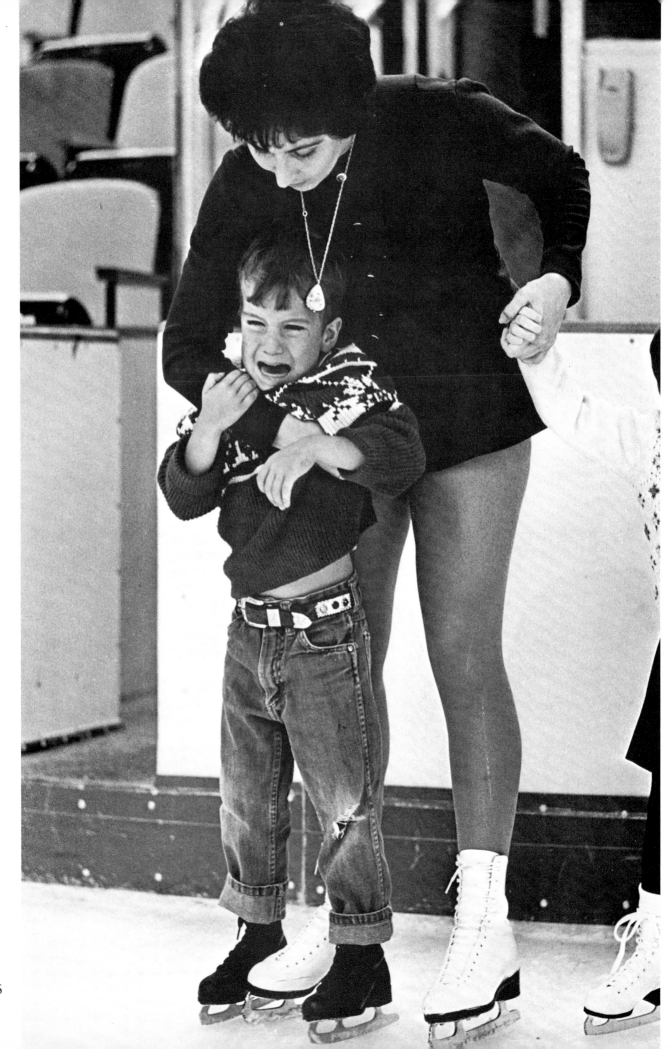

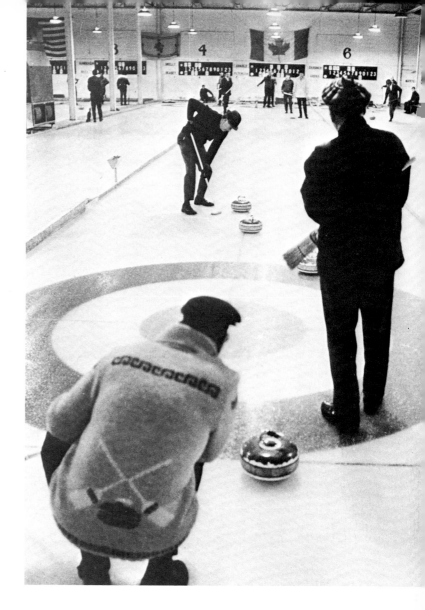

Ice is a versatile playground. Facing page: A young figure-skating student at the Metropolitan Sports Center in Bloomington. Ice is also for curling, an ancient Scottish sport imported into the northern United States from Canada. The game is not unlike shuffleboard, except that the markers are 42-pound stones with handles, and partners help maneuver them into the target area by briskly sweeping the ice with brooms. The competition shown here took place at the St. Paul Curling Club.

A farmer near Centerville gives children an old-fashioned bobsled ride.

Backpackers take to the woods in a park southwest of the Twin Cities.

Skiers on a double chair lift at Buck Hill, near the Twin Cities.

A farmer feeds white-tailed deer near Tofte, on the edge of Superior National Forest.

Though outnumbered by fishermen, Minnesota hunters have a variety of targets. Right, a young sportsman stalks ringnecked pheasants in a cornfield near Waseca. Below, a hunter wades through deep snow in the Arrowhead country toward his prize, a downed bull moose. There is an annual deer season, but moose, the biggest of the state's big game, have been hunted only rarely, and under sharply limited permits.

Wolf tracks on a snow-covered lake in the northern boundary waters area.

The Bell Museum of Natural History at the University of Minnesota gives youngsters a chance to touch and feel its exhibits. Above, a three-year-old puts on a wolfskin. Right, a traveling exhibit allows an elementary school student in Osseo to examine a turkey skeleton.

*The Winter Carnival is an annual St. Paul festival. The weather is
cold enough to turn a downtown street into a skating rink and keep
a masked Vulcan, the god of fire and warmth, in overshoes.*

*Hot air balloon races (above) are a feature of the Winter Carnival,
as are ice-fishing contests. Below, one way to keep
warm while angling for prizes.*

There are lots of ways to take fish. Above, winter fishermen lunch comfortably in an ice house on Lake Minnetonka. The man on the right is checking his line. Facing page: Top, fishermen open the summer, or iceless, season, at Lake Mille Lacs. Below, smelt fishing at the mouth of the French River near Duluth. During the spring smelt run, the tiny fish enter Lake Superior streams in such numbers they can be caught in dip nets. Night is the preferred time to take them.

Left, a canoe party starts down the Mississippi in the Twin Cities. Above, a canoe outing on the Cannon River in southern Minnesota.

Young fishermen curing their catch in an improvised smokehouse.

Above, a campground near Elk River. Below,
these houseboat tourists, with motorcycles lashed to the stern,
had chugged upriver from Illinois to the Twin Cities.

139

The Mississippi River begins as a tiny brook flowing out of Lake Itasca in northern Minnesota. Here it can be crossed on stepping stones. Facing page: The many small streams draining the Arrowhead country drop swiftly toward Lake Superior. In their rush they form waterfalls and rapids. This is Gooseberry Falls, northeast of Two Harbors.

A kayak racer paddles through rapids on the St. Croix River near Taylors Falls.
Facing page: Top, Split Rock Cliff and Lighthouse on Lake Superior's North Shore
in a rare winter air view. Below, Sand Dunes State Forest, between St. Cloud and
Minneapolis, is an unusual feature of central Minnesota's hill and lake country.

Under a darkening sky, sailboats compete in a regatta at Leech Lake in north central Minnesota.

Youngsters race boats made of milk cartons in a Minneapolis Aquatennial competition.

Young sailors nearly capsize in a brisk wind.
Below, when there's no wind, things aren't so lively.
The becalmed boats are on Lake Pepin.

Members of a crew strain at their oars during a race on
the Mississippi. Below, a water skier sends up a sheet of spray
during Minneapolis Aquatennial competition.

Golf is sometimes a relatively private affair, as in this league play at the Minnesota Valley Country Club. Below, sometimes it attracts a crowd, as in the 1970 U.S. Open at Hazeltine in suburban Chaska. (Tony Jacklin, a Briton, won.)

Parking-lot tailgate parties at Metropolitan Stadium in Bloomington. This pre-game combination of cocktail party and picnic (occasionally with music) is one which Minnesotans feel they originated—or at least raised to a new level of sophistication.

Alan Page, Vikings defensive tackle, collars Detroit Quarterback Bill Munson in a National Football Conference game. The 1973 Vikings won the National Conference title but lost to the Miami Dolphins in the Super Bowl.

Minnesota raises its own hockey players, from peewee teams to the high school squads which compete annually in the nation's biggest state prep tournament. Above, Edina and Bemidji teams in the 1972 meet. The program paid a special dividend in 1974 when the university won its first National Collegiate Athletic Association hockey title with a team made up entirely of Minnesota players. Most major U.S. college teams recruit Canadian players. Below, the 1974 Gopher team returns home after its victory in Boston.

*Minnesotans are resourceful at devising new pastimes to cope with
the long winters. One of them is racing cars on frozen lakes. Here racers make
the slush fly on St. Paul's Lake Phalen. Stock cars also compete.*

Facing page: Stanislaw Skrowaczewski, Polish-born conductor of the Minnesota Orchestra, formerly the Minneapolis Symphony. During its regular subscription season the orchestra plays weekly concerts at halls in both Minneapolis and St. Paul. The orchestra also makes regional, national, and international tours. Right, suburban schoolchildren watch a play performed by a touring group from the University of Minnesota Theatre. The late Sir Tyrone Guthrie (below) founded a regional repertory theater in Minneapolis that has achieved national distinction.

Valentina Perayaslavec drills ballet students at the Minnesota Dance Theatre in Minneapolis.

Top, George Morrison, Minnesota-born Chippewa artist, stands before a wood collage. Left, Minneapolis painter Jerry Ott and a painting done in his "super-realist" style. With the help of grants from state and federal arts programs, Patrick Redmond (above) became artist-in-residence at Eagle Bend, in the central part of the state. He worked mostly with public school students, here helps a member of an adult class.

The heart of Minnesota beats in full view at the annual State Fair, held in St. Paul and billed as the nation's largest. Farmers enter their prize livestock and grain, homemakers their cakes, preserves, and needlework. There are horse shows, art shows, outdoor concerts, wildlife exhibits, and industrial displays. Grandstand shows compete with amusements on the midway. The fair traces its roots back to 1855, and its cheerful hustle-bustle now attracts more than a million visitors each year.

A Future Farmer of America (above) *studies a hog. Below, a weight-guessing stand.*

Above, roller coaster ride. Below, cattle and their owners head for the judging ring.

157

Left, milk in the traditional way from an untraditional source, a plastic cow. Above, candidates for the title of Princess Kay, a dairy promotion, go aloft on the Space Needle.

When you win prizes this big on the midway, it's time to head for home.